TO: Athalia smith

Please share my message
"We are better together"!

Mariah Cubano

Follow my Journey @Riah_way

Riah's Way

presents

I'VE BEEN TOLD

written by Mariah Cubano
illustrated by Subi Bosa

ISBN: 978-0-578-85191-4
Copyright 2021 Mariah Cubano

I dedicate this book to my oldest brother,
David Bon Kartelli,
who always told me to believe in myself
and my capabilities.

Thank you, David,
for always loving and
guiding me.

I love and miss you
so much.

This is for you!

I've been told...

But no matter what you call me,

African-American, young girl...

with the **PUFFY** hair.

Teased since I was 3
by kids who look different than me.

Taught by my parents...

...to be **PROUD,**
LOVE WHO I AM
and STAND **TALL**

Even if...

...I'm different

than them all.

I continued to grow my inner strength, by loving who I am and knowing **I'M ALWAYS ENOUGH!**

I couldn't allow hate to win

and I ask all who are listening
to do the same.

HATE

HATE

HATE

Don't allow **HATE** to fill your heart,

because we're all **BETTER TOGETHER**, not apart!

because LOVE WINS
when we're kind
to one another!

Finally, I want to end with this...

I'm **THANKFULL**

to all my **African-American**
ancestors and to all who helped
end slavery and segregation
so I never have to go through that.

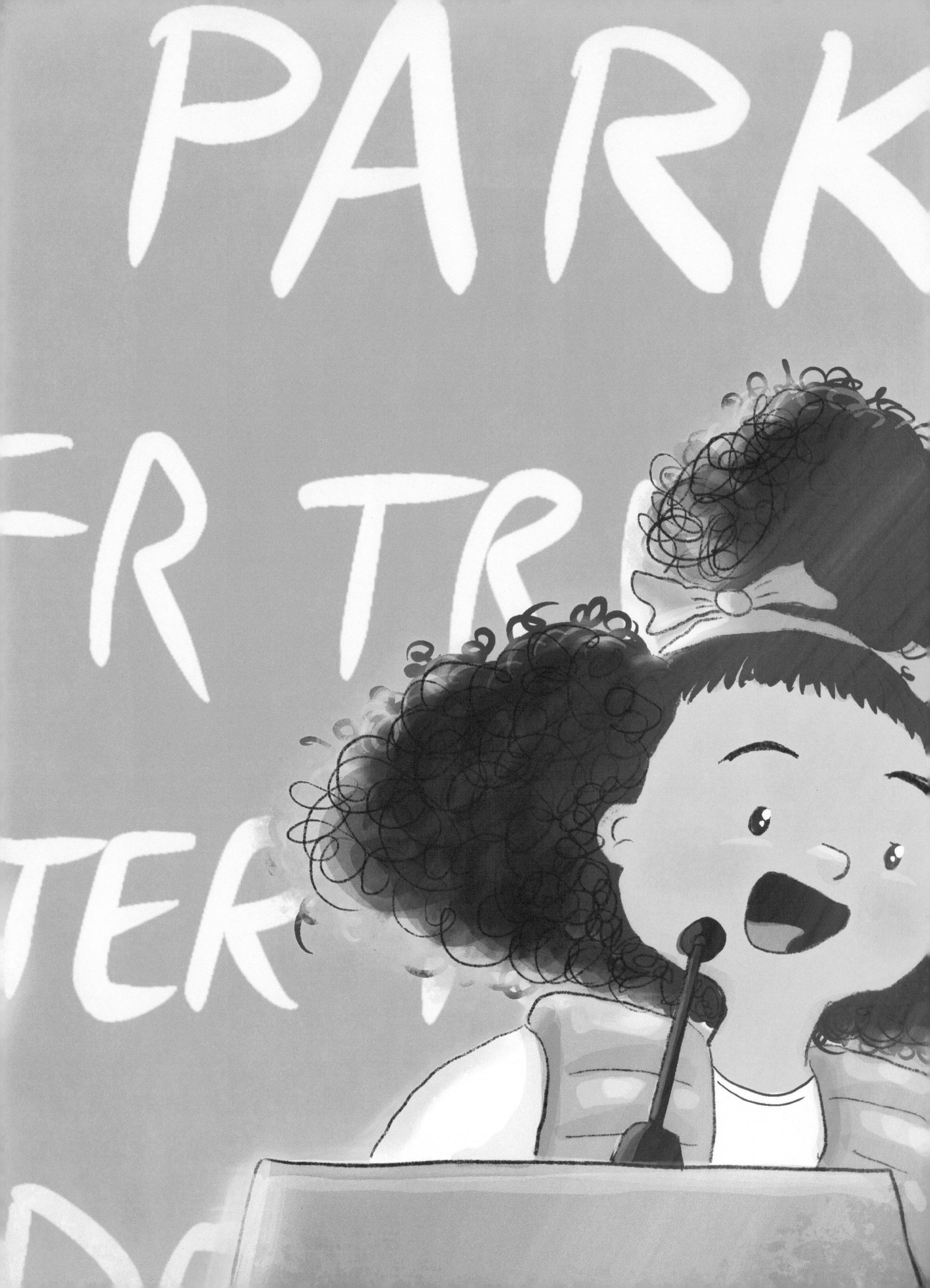

PARK
ER TR
TER

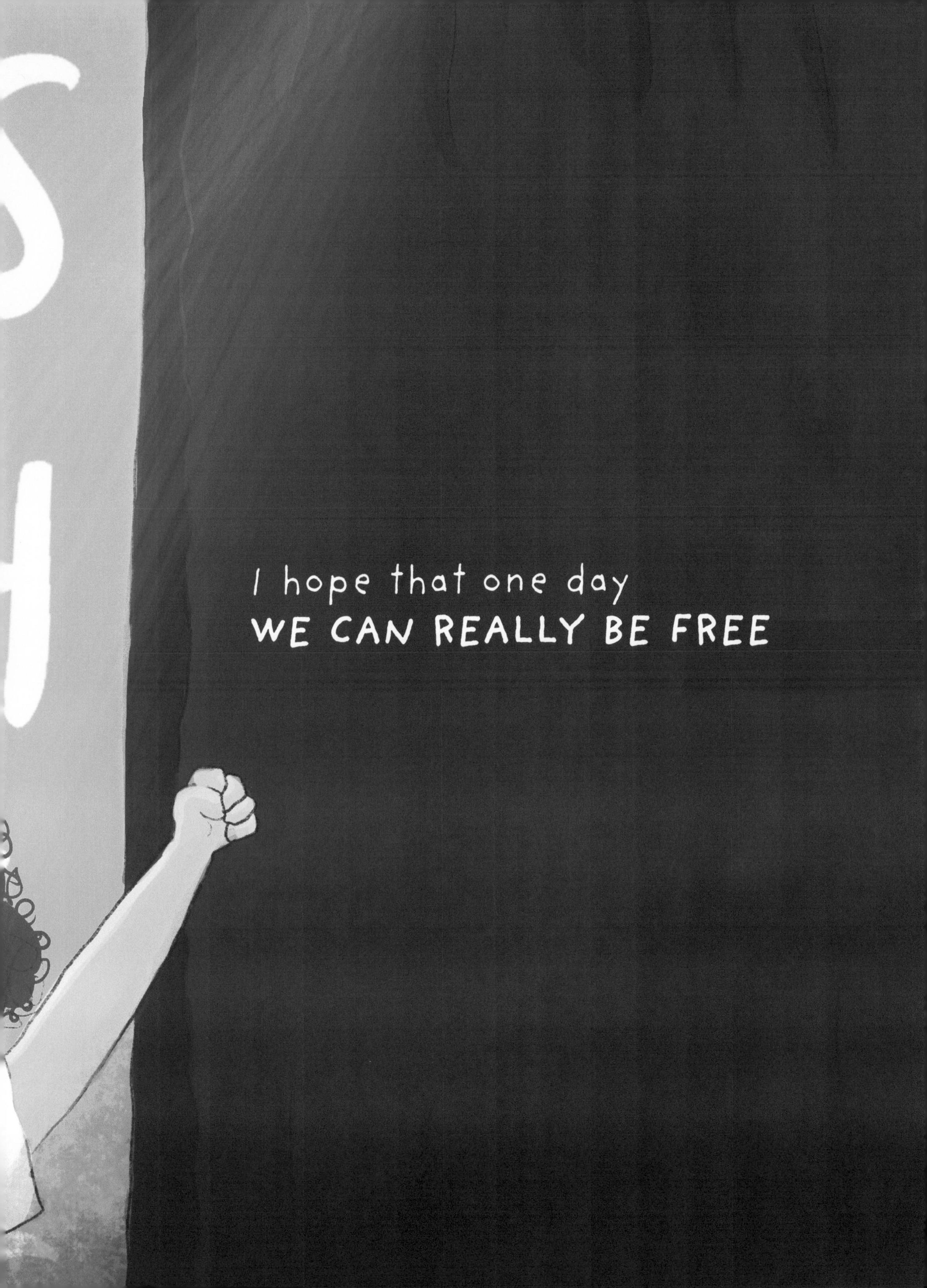
I hope that one day
WE CAN REALLY BE FREE

and not be judged
by the color of our skin!

Please show **LOVE**
and teach **LOVE** because...

I MATTER,

YOU MATTER,